Nadine O'Shea

Preventing A New Cold War – Why Realpolitik still matters

Why the relations between Russia and Western countries are tense, who is responsible for the Ukraine crisis and how the crisis could be solved

Anchor Academic Publishing

O'Shea, Nadine: Preventing A New Cold War – Why Realpolitik still matters. Why the relations between Russia and Western countries are tense, who is responsible for the Ukraine crisis and how the crisis could be solved, Hamburg, Anchor Academic Publishing 2017

Buch-ISBN: 978-3-96067-182-4
PDF-eBook-ISBN: 978-3-96067-682-9
Druck/Herstellung: Anchor Academic Publishing, Hamburg, 2017

Bibliografische Information der Deutschen Nationalbibliothek:
Die Deutsche Nationalbibliothek verzeichnet diese Publikation in der Deutschen Nationalbibliografie; detaillierte bibliografische Daten sind im Internet über http://dnb.d-nb.de abrufbar.

Bibliographical Information of the German National Library:
The German National Library lists this publication in the German National Bibliography. Detailed bibliographic data can be found at: http://dnb.d-nb.de

All rights reserved. This publication may not be reproduced, stored in a retrieval system or transmitted, in any form or by any means, electronic, mechanical, photocopying, recording or otherwise, without the prior permission of the publishers.

Das Werk einschließlich aller seiner Teile ist urheberrechtlich geschützt. Jede Verwertung außerhalb der Grenzen des Urheberrechtsgesetzes ist ohne Zustimmung des Verlages unzulässig und strafbar. Dies gilt insbesondere für Vervielfältigungen, Übersetzungen, Mikroverfilmungen und die Einspeicherung und Bearbeitung in elektronischen Systemen.

Die Wiedergabe von Gebrauchsnamen, Handelsnamen, Warenbezeichnungen usw. in diesem Werk berechtigt auch ohne besondere Kennzeichnung nicht zu der Annahme, dass solche Namen im Sinne der Warenzeichen- und Markenschutz-Gesetzgebung als frei zu betrachten wären und daher von jedermann benutzt werden dürften.

Die Informationen in diesem Werk wurden mit Sorgfalt erarbeitet. Dennoch können Fehler nicht vollständig ausgeschlossen werden und die Diplomica Verlag GmbH, die Autoren oder Übersetzer übernehmen keine juristische Verantwortung oder irgendeine Haftung für evtl. verbliebene fehlerhafte Angaben und deren Folgen.

Alle Rechte vorbehalten

© Anchor Academic Publishing, Imprint der Diplomica Verlag GmbH
Hermannstal 119k, 22119 Hamburg
http://www.diplomica-verlag.de, Hamburg 2017
Printed in Germany

Abstract

This paper reviews multiple views of the origins of the current crisis in Ukraine and it argues that Realpolitik still matters to some countries. For this, several reasons will be given. One has to understand not only the history of Ukraine, in order to understand the crisis, but also what interest western countries and Russia have in Ukraine. Furthermore, it is crucial to know what interest the Ukrainian government and its population have in the EU, NATO or in Russia. Analyzing the relationship between western countries and Russia after the Cold War will help to comprehensively understand Russia´s view of the conflict as well as the competing views of the EU and NATO. Ukraine is heavily affected by the actions of those states and organizations, but it is an active state which could immensely contribute to a solution. Hence, this paper will analyze how Ukraine itself can contribute to end the crisis. Furthermore, this paper analyses why finger-pointing is not helpful to find a solution. Finally, the paper offers solutions and to the crisis which have been analyzed among other alternatives. Throughout the paper, there will be arguments in favor and against the statement that Realpolitik still matters and has to be considered in order to prevent a new Cold War.

Table of Contents

1. INTRODUCTION 3

2. UKRAINE – A COUNTRY WITH DIVERSITY 4
   - 2.1. Facts about the Ukraine 4
   - 2.2. History of Ukraine and major events of the current Ukraine crisis 4

3. A TENSE RELATIONSHIP BETWEEN WESTERN COUNTRIES AND RUSSIA 8
   - 3.1. The relations between the West and Russia after the Cold War 8
   - 3.2. Escalation of the conflict – the Ukrainian crisis 9
     - 3.2.1. Russia´s Realpolitik versus EU and NATO enlargement and what it means for Ukraine 9
     - 3.2.2. National Identity crisis in Ukraine 18

4. WHO IS TO BLAME FOR THE UKRAINE CRISIS AND DOES FINGER-POINTING MAKE SENSE TO SOLVE THE CRISIS? 21

5. WHAT NEEDS TO BE DONE TO SOLVE THE UKRAINE CRISIS 23

6. CONCLUSION 26

REFERENCES 30

1. Introduction

The Ukraine crisis and Russia´s aggressive behavior was surprising for many state. Many people get killed, the fights are continuing and a first ceasefire agreement was violated. Currently, there seems to be little hope for peace in Ukraine in the near future. This papers argues that, however, that western countries have to change their behavior. This is not because Russia´s point of view is right or understandable, it is absolutely not. Western countries need to change because that is the only way to find a solution to the crisis. Russia feels threatened by NATO and EU expansion and this will not change soon. Only if western countries accept that to Russia geopolitics is in its national interests, then they will be able to find a solution. This will also have a positive effect on Ukraine´s national identity, because the Ukrainian government or the Ukrainian population will not feel being pulled to one side or another. It will be able to unite as a nation and to prevent aggressive behavior by other states. Section 2.1 will state facts about Ukraine to see why geopolitics is important and why Ukraine as difficulty of finding its national identity. Section 2.2 analyses the history of Ukraine and summarizes the major events of the crisis in Ukraine. This section is important in order to gain a comprehensive understanding of the Ukrainian crisis. It is crucial to see the development of Ukraine, its history and its relations towards other countries over the past years. That way, the complexity of the crisis can be understood. Section 3.1 describes the relation between western countries and Russia after the Cold War and it analyses the development of the relationship. Section 3.2.2 argues that to Russia Realpolitik is still important and thus, Russia does not agree with NATO or EU expansion. It furthermore states how Realpolitik affects Ukraine. Section 3.2.3 analyses why Ukraine seems to be divided into west and east Ukraine and how this contributes to the crisis. For the finding of a solution to the crisis, this question of Ukraine´s national identity is extremely important that it deserves an own section which will analyze Ukraine´s national identity problem in more details. In section 4, it will be analyzed who is responsible for the crisis and if knowing this contributes to a solution to the crisis. Section 5 analyses different views of how to solve the crisis in Ukraine. Finally, section 6 finalizes the research and answers the research question. It will therefore answer why Realpolitik still matters and what can be done to solve the crisis.

2. Ukraine – a country with diversity

2.1. Facts about the Ukraine

Ukraine is the largest country within Europe, surrounded by Russia, Moldova, Romania, Slovakia, Hungary, Poland, Belarus and Russia and with the Black Sea as its natural boundary in the south (Consulate General of Ukraine in New York, 2007). It is home to approximately 44.740.000 people. This population is diverse, consisting of 78% Ukrainians, 17% Russians and 0.5% Tartars. The official language is Ukrainian, however, Russian is also widely spoken, especially in the Southern and Eastern parts of Ukraine. The system of government in Ukraine is a parliamentary-presidential republic with different political parties. There are 24 counties in Ukraine and due to recent developments, the peninsula Crimea is an autonomous republic. Ukraine is member to various international organizations, among others to the United Nations, International Labor Organization, International Monetary Fund and the World Trade Organization. The media is widely spread within the Ukraine, therefore there are many private as well as public TV channels and newspapers (German Ministry of Foreign Affairs, 2014).

2.2. History of Ukraine and major events of the current Ukraine crisis

Today´s capital of Ukraine, Kiev, is seen as a birth place of Russia by many Ukrainians and Russians. In the 9th century, Keivan Rus was a prosperous East Slavic Federation. With the invasion of the Mongols in the 12th century, Keivan Rus was dissolved. The Russian Empire annexed northern parts of Kuvein Rus whereas most Ukrainian regions were dominated by the Poland-Lithuanian Commonwealth in the 1386 century. In the 16th century, Russia and Poland-Lithuanian Commonwealth fought about Ukraine and its borders. Some Ukrainians fled to the center of the Ukraine and formed a militant group called Cossacks. The Ukrainian population found to be secure under the Cossacks and protected against the oppression by Poland-Lithuanian Commonwealth. In the 17th century, a war between Ukraine and Poland-Lithuanian Commonwealth broke out which was won by Ukraine with the help of its Russian ally. Afterwards, Ukraine was taken in by the Russian Empire with the idea that Ukraine would mainly be independent from Russia. However, the Russian Empire started to limit Ukrainian´s right immediately. Later in the 17th century, Ukraine was divided as a result of the Russian-Polish war. The Russian Empire occupied Eastern Ukraine whereas Poland acquired Western Ukraine. Throughout the war, the Cossacks tried to free Ukraine from Russia, unsuccessfully. In the early 19th century, Russia prohibited the Ukrainian language and symbols. In order to protect Ukrainians national heritage, the Ukrainian population mobilized itself against the Russian

Empire. With the Revolution of 1905, the Russian government had to give certain rights to the Ukrainians and it was even represented in the Duma, Russia´s legislative institution. During the First World War, Ukraine suffered terribly by being between the two confronting countries. Many Ukrainians were fighting in the Russian army. Others, however, were joining Austrian forces. During this time, the first military Ukrainian army was established under the Supreme Ukrainian Council, fighting for an independent Ukraine. In 1915, Ukraine was again divided into East and West. Austria acquired West Ukraine While Russia occupied East Ukraine. Pro-Russian Ukrainians suffered from oppression by Austria, Ukrainians in East Ukraine were completely oppressed by Russia. Following economic, social and political crisis with terrible consequences to the population in the Russian Empire, the Revolution of 1917 started. Tsar Nicholas II was abdicated and the Russian Empire was ended. During this time, Ukrainians established their own governmental institutions and stopped the ban on the Ukrainian language and symbols. In 1918, the Ukraine declared its independence. However, Poland and Soviet Russia conquered Ukraine and distributed its regions between them. Poland gained West Ukraine and Russia acquired East Ukraine, including Crimea, and some regions were occupied by Romania and Czechoslovakia. In 1922, the Soviet Socialist Republics of Ukraine and Russia became the founding members of the Soviet Union which was controlled by Russia. During World War Two, Germany invaded the Ukraine which resulted in great economic and human losses. A famine occurred in Soviet Ukraine due to a food shortage. This famine is now seen by the Ukraine as genocide carried out by Stalin and other high-ranking Soviet officials. The occupation ended in 1944, leaving a devastated Ukraine behind. In 1954, Crimea was given to Ukraine by Russia. The Soviet Union dissolved in 1990 and Ukraine gained independence (Jenkins, B., 2014). With the end of the Union of Soviet Social Republics, those republics established an association called the Commonwealth of Independent States. Its treaty ensures the equality and independence of the member states and the recognition of sovereignty. Furthermore, the treaty states the importance of intensifying the relations between the member states (OECD, 2013). The first president, Leonid Kravchuk, was democratically elected. He tried to maintain Ukrainian´s independence and sovereignty (Berkely Center, 2014). The second president of the Ukraine, Leonid Kuchma, was elected (BBC, 2014). In 1997, Ukraine and Russia signed the Black Sea Fleet Agreement which gave Russia the approval to move its troops in Crimea. According to the agreement, Russia had to respect Ukraine´s law and could only move its troops by respecting Ukraine´s sovereignty (Zadorozhny, et al, 2014). After President Kuchma was accused for corruption, the population protested in 2002 and demanded his resignation. In 2004, the presidential election between Yanukovych, who was rather Pro-Russia oriented, and Yushenko, a rather Pro-European politician, took place. In the run-off vote, Yanukovych won the election. This election, however, was under the shadow of fraud and Yanukovych was accused of rigging it. Massive protests followed, demanding the annulation of the result. Ukraine´s Supreme Court agreed and a second run-off was introduced, in which Yushenko succeeded over Yanukovych. This period is also called the Orange Revolution. In the following years, Ukraine had dramatic difficulties to supply its country with gas since its main gas supplier, Russia, cut off the supply. In 2010, Yanukovych was elected for presidency. He extended the Black Sea Fleet Agreement with Russia in return for cheaper gas supplies by Russia. In the same year, former Prime Minister of Ukraine, is found guilty over an illegal gas deal with Russia and was imprisoned in 2009. The EU, among others, said that the charges were politically motivated and therefore illegal. Moreover, many head of states refused to visit the Euro 2012 football championship and the summit in Yalta in response to the imprisonment and mistreatment of Tymoshenko (BBC, 2014). The Law on the Principles of the state language policy was introduced, declaring Russian a regional language in its jurisdictions in Ukraine. This evoked mass protests which often ended up violently. This law was seen to divide the country into East and West again because Russian-speaking people were discouraged from learning Ukrainian (The Guardian, 2012). In 2013, the European Court of Human Rights stated the arrest of Tymoshenko as illegal (ECHR, 2013). In the same year, Ukraine and the EU were preparing the EU Association Agreement which would have resulted in closer economic and political ties between the EU and Ukraine. Furthermore, the Ukrainian population would have greatly benefited. According to the EU High Representative Catherine Ashton, Ukraine would have experienced prosperity through reforms and modernization (Ashton, C., 2013) However, the EU set up a condition for Ukraine in order to be able to sign the EU Association Agreement. Ukraine would have to allow former PM Tymoshenko to leave the country due to health reasons. President Yanukovych did not fulfilled this condition (BBC, 2014). Furthermore, Yanukovych refused to sign the EU Association Agreement saying that the EU did not provide enough financial help. Prior to this, Russia decreased its imports to Ukraine. This was seen as pressuring the Ukraine into Russia´s Customs Union. Yanukovych stated that Ukraine could not give up its ties to Russia (Rutland. P, 2013). This was followed by mass protests in Ukraine, starting on the Independence Square, also known as Maidan Square. Those demonstrations were later called "Euro Maidan" (Balmfroth. R, 2012). Ukrainians in favour of the EU Association Agreement blocked governmental buildings and demanded closer ties with the EU. Various violent clashes between protestors and police forces occurred (BBC, 2013). By February 2013, many protestors were killed. The Ukrainian president Yanukovych escaped to Russia. Ukraine´s opposition set up an interim government with the interim president Turchynov. While the US and the EU recognized the election and the interim president, Russia did not (Herszenhorn, D.M

2014). In the same month, Pro-Russian Ukrainians protested in Sevastopol, the capital of the Crimea peninsula, demanding to join the Russian Federation (Siddique, H. et al., 2014). Crimea´s parliament held a referendum which was neither recognized by the US, nor by the EU or Ukraine. It was, however, recognized by Russia. The result of the referendum showed that the Crimean population wanted to join the Russian Federation. During this time, Russian troops were seen to move from the Russian fleet in the Black Sea on to the territory of Crimea, which was still territory of Ukraine. Later, Russia´s president Putin visited Sevastopol to celebrate Crimea´s decision to join the Russian Federation. Russia defended its invasion into Crimea by saying that Russia needed to protect the Russian-speaking minority in Ukraine. The US and the EU held Russia responsible for pushing the referendum. Sanctions against Russia followed (Morello, C., 2014). The US and the EU claimed that Russia was violating international law by annexing Crimea and ignoring Ukraine´s sovereignty and territorial integrity (The White House, 2014). Moreover, Russia sent troops close to the Ukrainian border (Vertretungen der BRD in der russischen Förderation, 2014). The US and the EU considered that Russia would invade the Ukraine (Campbell, C., 2014). Protests in East Ukraine, Donetsk and Donbass, followed in which Pro-Russians demanded that those regions would also join the Russian Federation. The US and the EU accused Russia of supporting Pro-Russian separatists (Baczynska, G. et al, 2014). In May 2014, the Ukraine voted Poroshenko for president who is in favor of closer ties with the EU (Birnbaum, M. et al, 2014). Poroshenko signs the EU Association Agreement (BBC, 2014). In July 2014, a Malaysian commercial airliner was shot down above Ukrainian territory, killing all passengers. The US accused not Russia directly but they did accuse Pro-Russian separatists, which are supported by the Russian Federation, to shut down the airliner with a missile. The US government demanded an independent investigation (Shear, M. et al, 2014). In September 2014, the Minsk protocol was introduced. This peace agreement was signed by Ukraine, the Russian Federation and the regions of Donetsk and Donbass, calling for a ceasefire and dialogues (Ministry of Foreign Affairs of Ukraine, 2014). However, the ceasefire has been violated. Furthermore, Russian troops were seen on Ukrainian territory. In Donbass, war continued. Parliamentary elections were held in Ukraine but hindered by Pro-Russian separatists. They tried to ensure their power within the region and were thereby violating the Minsk agreement (BBC, 2014). The current situation in Ukraine is according to the United Nations and Amnesty International a humanitarian crisis. Especially, the population suffers and there are many internally displaced persons. The Ukrainian government cut off its public services in region ruled by Pro-Russian separatists. Ukrainian´s strategy is to keep the population away from the separatists and turning to the legitimate Ukrainian government (Golinkin, L., 2014).

3. A tense relationship between western countries and Russia

3.1. The relations between the West and Russia after the Cold War

The official end of the Cold War in 1991 and the reunification of Germany gave hope for a new and peaceful world order. After a time of oppression and centralized authority within the Soviet Union by Stalin, Gorbachev became the last president of the Soviet Union. He was following new ideas which focused towards democratization, liberalization and non-violence, Gorbachev´s domestic and foreign politics were very different than Stalin´s. Gorbachev desired peaceful co-existence. However, under his leadership, the Soviet Union was economically weak. Gorbachev was rather Western-oriented and communist ideas, which he still had in the beginning of his presidency, decreased. In 1988, he was preparing a speech about his new way of thinking, also called Perestroika, for the General Assembly of the United Nations. Gorbachev believed in good partnership with the US and other Western countries and kept friendly relationships with the former US president Reagan and former chancellor of West-Germany Kohl. Many scholars agree that the end of the Cold War was possible because of Gorbachev´s policies and positive attitudes towards Western countries (Zubok, V.M., 2007). For the states of the former Soviet Union, the end of the Cold War meant redefining their national identity. Now those states were not centrally controlled by Moscow anymore. They needed to define and establish their new institutions and policies which was a big challenge. Russia´s territory thereby decreased immensely and it was concerned with its neighbor countries. Even though, the Soviet Union dissolved, Russia´s way of thinking in communist terms did not disappear immediately. This was the main obstacle for the relations between Russia and Western countries (Kissinger, H. 1994). Gorbachev had many opponents who did not agree with his Western-oriented politics (Zubok, V.M. 2007). However, directly after the Cold War, Western countries cooperated and assisted states of the former Soviet Union. In 1992, the US and Russia agreed on the reduction of strategic arms. Germany and Russia proposed to establish an international center for science and technology. Several declarations of US-Russian cooperation followed. In 1997, the NATO-Russia Founding Act was created through which states declared that they do not consider each other as adversaries anymore. Instead, they were working on cooperation, democracy and followed the approach to gain European security. In 2000, Russia and the US had different views on how to solve the crisis in the Balkans and in the Persian Gulf. However, in general there was cooperation and the countries used its diplomatic channels (US Department of State, 2009). In 2001, the Russian president Putin gave his first speech in the German parliament. He honored the Russian-German partnership which was always important throughout history. Putin mentioned that the Cold War is over and next steps towards a peaceful and secure Europe have to be taken. A first step towards security was the START II agreement for arms reduction, however, Putin critized that not all NATO members followed the agreement. In his speech he generally critizes NATO by saying that there is no real partnership between Russia and NATO. Often, Russia has not the possibility to participate in the decision-making of NATO but NATO demands Russia´s loyalty. Putin claimed that this is not an effective partnership. Without real partnership, however, it would not be possible to gain mutual trust. Thus, it would not be possible to provide security throughout Europe (Putin, W. 2001). The ineffective partnership between Russia and the West, especially NATO, was also mentioned by Nikolay Patrushev, Secretary of the Russian Security Council in 2014. Patrushev claimed that in 2008 for the first time after the end of the Cold War, the US government supported a foreign government, namely Georgia, which has oppressed and attacked its Russian citizens. The same is true for the Russian minority in Ukraine which eventually led to the current crisis. It is obvious that Russian´s interests are different from the interests of Western countries. Even though the end of the Cold War gave hope for future peace and stability, the crisis in Ukraine reminds people of the era of the Cold War during which mutual mistrust existed and people were uncertain of the other state´s action (Patrushev, N.).

3.2. Escalation of the conflict – the Ukrainian crisis

3.2.1. Russia´s Realpolitik versus EU and NATO enlargement and what it means for Ukraine

From early beginnings of Russian history, the country had shifting borders and often struggled to control its diverse population. Furthermore, Russia never had clear security plans, those plans changed depending on circumstances. During the Cold War, now independent states belonged to the Soviet Union and were controlled by Moscow. The ideologies of Russia and the West were very different and both countries thought that they could not properly co-exist because their ideologies, communist Russia and the capitalistic West, were incompatible. With the end of the Cold War, people thought that the countries differences would not matter anymore. The US hoped that geopolitics would also not be as important to Russia anymore (Kissinger, 1994). NATO and Russia tried to build up a partnership and established the North Atlantic Cooperation Council for consultation of which Russia became a member in 1992, and the Partnership for Peace was established in 1994. However, whenever NATO was discussing NATO enlargement, Russia was opposed it. Signing NATO agreements and agreements towards more cooperation between Russia and NATO was often seen as an approval by Russia for NATO enlargement. This assumption was a mistake because Russia always considered an expansion by NATO eastwards as intervening into Russia´s area of influence. Russia saw NATO´s potential, and thus perceived it as a threat, because it has influence on high-security problems (Allison,R., 2006). After the collapse of the Soviet Union and the end of the Cold War, western countries, such as the US and the EU, focused on democracy, liberalization, globalization and cooperation. National interests were still important but economic interdependence made conflicts less likely. They did not consider that the idea of Realpolitik, in which countries want to gain power through strategic geopolitics, would still be important in the post-Cold War era. The current conflict in Ukraine, however, shows that for some countries, Realpolitik is an important subject and even more important than moral values or international law. To Russia, Realpolitik still matters. It wants to protect national interests, which is its own survival, by maximizing its own power. Thus, Russia does not want its former territories and its neighbors, such as Ukraine, to become a member of NATO or EU. Those Western organizations would threaten Russia and decrease its influence over Ukraine. Russia demands to maintain its regional power and its position as the regional hegemon. All this would be decreasing if Ukraine would become a member of NATO or EU. Knowing this, western countries need to reconsider the idea of Realpolitik and how to deal with countries to whom this is still important, even in the post-Cold War era (Arun, S., 2015). Some scholars state that Russia is the only country that is unwilling to accept the sovereignty of states which belonged to the Russian Empire and then to the Soviet Union under Russian control before. Hence, Russia is unwilling to overcome its colonial powers and to accept those countries´ sovereignty. It tries to preserve its former powers as an empire (Vasecka, M., 2015). Other scholars argue that Russia´s behavior of trying to influence smaller states is nothing new and common in states´ foreign policies. Since Russia is a great power, it tries to influence smaller countries in an advantageous way for Russia. However, this is the case for all great powers, hence the US also tries to influence smaller states. The only aspect special for Russia is that it still tries to have a buffer-zone between itself and NATO member states, which is similar to the situation during the Cold War and shows again that Russia´s geopolitical interests have not changed with the collapse of the Soviet Union (Kansikas, S., 2015). Russia might not want to rebuild former structures of the Russian Empire of the Soviet Union in which Moscow controlled different states and ethnic groups, but Russia wants to defend its national interests (Simons, G., 2015). Immediately after the Cold War, Russia was concerned with the former Soviet countries and its neighbors. Ukraine was and still is a country of Russia´s special interest because it served as a "buffer zone" between Russia and Europe as well as between Russia and NATO. Ukraine and Russia share an important strategic region, the Black Sea, which is of special interest to Russia and Ukraine as well as to NATO. Russia, on the other hand, is vital for Ukraine since it buys its energy from Russia. The US and the EU are crucial for Ukraine because it gets financial and technical help from them which contributes to European security. Russia as well as western countries are important for Ukraine, but Ukraine struggles with being in between the two sides. Ukrainian politicians and the Ukrainian population are also for these reasons divided. Some prefer Ukrainian policies to be more western-oriented whereas others would like policies to be rather Russia-oriented. Within the past years, Ukrainian policies shifted according to the then governing party and president towards either the EU and US or Russia. However, only in the year 2000, Ukraine had signed about 200 agreements and projects with NATO. The Russian population and its politicians were upset about this. The Ukrainian foreign minister, Tarasyuk, tried to ease the anger by saying that Ukraine would not join NATO in the near future. However, this did not work and Russia promised to watch the relations between Ukraine and NATO closely (Black, J.L., 2004). One might ask why the partnership with NATO is so crucial for Ukraine and vice versa. Would it not be better for Ukraine to give up its close partnership with NATO in order to ease the tension it has with Russia? NATO supports Ukraine with technical assistance and with defense and security reforms through which Ukraine's capacity for defense shall increase. Moreover, NATO cooperates with Ukraine for civil emergencies and disaster preparedness. NATO, on the other hand, respects Ukraine because it contributes to NATO projects and peace operations led by NATO. It supports Ukraine because a stable Ukraine is crucial for Euro-Atlantic security. Since 1997, the relation between NATO and Ukraine developed due to dialogue and cooperation (NATO, 2014). However, this partnership is perceived as a threat by Russia. The American scholar and professor at the University of Chicago, John J. Mearsheimer, best known as an advocate for offensive realism, wrote several essays about the events in Ukraine. He argues that Russia perceives NATO enlargement, especially when including its neighbors, as a threat because Russia fears that Ukraine is taken out of Russian influence and could be incorporated into the West. Russia's position towards NATO enlargement was clear since the 1990s, it officially said that it was opposed to NATO enlargement. Ukraine would be crucial to Russia for strategic reasons. Mearsheimer states that realism and Realpolitik is still important in international politics. The US and EU thought differently, promoted democracy, focused on the rule of law and other liberal concepts and ignored that other countries could follow the path of Realpolitik. Therefore, the US and EU is mostly responsible for the current crisis in Ukraine. Only some Western countries, like Germany and France, understood that to Russia, Realpolitik and geopolitics still matter. Thus, they were opposed Ukrainian NATO membership because this would provoke Russia and Russia would take action (Mearsheimer, J.J., 2014). Other scholars go even further and compare Russia's action with US actions in the past. Russia's annexation of Crimea was a violation against international law. However, US invasion of Iraq in 2003 was also a violation of international law. Both actions were not acceptable. The specific problem with the Ukraine crisis is that after the German Reunion, NATO and its members promised Russia that it would not expand beyond the former East-Germany. But, today there are missile defense systems close to Russian border. Furthermore, the West should be more sensible towards geopolitical issues because geopolitics does matter. Pradetto compares the NATO enlargement with the Cuban Missile Crisis in 1962 in which Russia installed middle-range missiles on Cuba. This was not acceptable for the US, because Cuba was too close to the US and this action was perceived as a threat against the US. Ukrainian membership in NATO would not be acceptable for Russia like the missiles, which were installed on Cuba by Russia during the Cold War, were not acceptable for the US (Pradetto, A., 2014). Furthermore, NATO was built to challenge the former Soviet Union, therefore, Putin´s feel of being threatened is to some extent rational since NATO still exist but the Soviet Union does not (Simons, G., 2015) Russian president Putin gave a speech at the Munich Conference on Security Policy in which he stated that NATO would be a threat for Russia. He also stated that with the dissolution of the Warsaw Pact and NATO membership of the reunited Germany, assurances and guarantees by NATO and its members were made, which declared that NATO would not expand beyond Germany. In 1999, Russia ratified the Adapted Treaty on Conventional Armed Forces in Europe and Russia faced a situation with new geopolitics. Even though Russia ratified and therefore hold its promise of ratifying the treaty, NATO did not hold its promise and did expand beyond Germany. Generally, NATO poses a threat to Russia because NATO would not have the character of the UN, for example, which would be universal in nature. Instead, NATO is firstly a military and political organization. Putin argued that since Russia would not pose a threat, there would be no need for NATO to expand towards Russia´s borders. He stated that not Russia is a threat to the world, but terrorism which has to be tackled together. Furthermore, Putin argues that Russia contributed to make an end to the Cold War, promoted democracy and freedom and NATO would only divide Europe (Putin, V. 2007). Whereas Putin felt that Russia was threatened by NATO expansion towards Russia´s borders, other countries could have perceived Russia´s actions as a threat, even before it annexed Crimea. In Putin´s speech to the Federal Assembly of the Russian Federation in 2013 he argues that Russia does not try to be a superpower, but a country which respects international law, sovereignty and independence. He refers to the Syrian crisis and states that international issues could only be solved through diplomacy, not with forceful actions. However, he does say that "No one should entertain any illusions about achieving military superiority over Russia; we will never allow it … We will have a lot to do to develop modern high-precision weapons systems. At the same time, judged by qualitative parameters for modern nuclear deterrent forces, today we are successfully reaching new milestones on schedule, and some of our partners will have to catch up. We are developing new strategic missile systems for land, sea and air to further strengthen our nuclear forces. We will continue to strengthen our nuclear missile forces and continue building a fleet of nuclear submarines (Putin, V., 2013). This does not only remind us of Cold War times but one could perceive this as aggressive behavior rather than defensive actions. Putin stated in his Annual Address to the Federal Assembly of the Russian Federation that the collapse of the Soviet Union was a geopolitical disaster because Russian people were, as a result, divided by borders. To others, however, Putin seems to be a Russian patriot, but he was willing to cooperate during several incidents. After the attacks on the World Trade Center in 2001, Russia was willing to share its intelligence with the US in order to find terrorists. Yet, to Russia Realpolitik becomes an important aspect whenever it fears that Russia´s power and influence on its neighbor countries could decrease. After president Yanukovych left Ukraine and Ukraine implemented an interim government with the support of the EU and the US, which Russia perceived as a coup, Russia thought it was time to act by invading a sovereign country and annexing parts of it. Yet, Russia already had great influence on Crimea, so there was no need to annex the peninsula. Putin saw Russia´s annexation of Crimea as defending Russian minorities, therefore, he did not see Russia´s action as aggressive but rather as defensive (Bowen, A.S. and Galeotti, M., 2014). Russia´s attempt to protect Russian minorities in foreign countries can explain Russia´s invasion into Ukraine, but it certainly does not justify it. However, Russia´s behavior makes clear that Realpolitik still matters and that geopolitical interests can result in crises and wars if they compete (Simons, G. 2015). Yet, Russia stated that it feels more threatened by NATO expansion than by EU expansion since NATO is a military and political organization whereas the EU is a universal organization. At the beginnings of the developments of the EU, the member states tried to make sure that Russia would not perceive the EU as a threat but rather as an organization which wishes to cooperate with Russia in order to achieve European peace and security. In 1997, Russia and the EU ratified the Partnership and Cooperation Agreement to promote democracy, freedom, peace and security throughout Europe. The goal was to achieve great cooperation and a closer relation between Russia and the EU which could also eventually lead to free trade between them. Even before the agreement, the EU supported Russia economically with the agreement on Technical Assistance to the Commonwealth, also Ukraine benefited from it. With this, EU member states tried to help former Soviet states with their transition into democracy and a free market economy. The idea was that stable and secure neighbors would strengthen the region as a whole. Moreover, Russia is an important trading partner to the EU which is supplying large amounts of energy and the EU is economically crucial to Russia because the EU accounted for 52% of Russia´s foreign trade compared with 3% with the US in 2005. Even though, the progress of EU-Russia relations was sometimes slow, generally there is an intense economic and political cooperation. Furthermore, the EU is important to Russia when relations between Russia and the US get tense, then the EU often acts as a mediator. Putin sees Russia as part of Europe and therefore, the EU is high on Russia´s foreign policy agenda. However, Putin is concerned with NATO enlargement as well as with EU enlargement. With both organizations, Russia fears that it is excluded from the decision-making process and thus, excluded from decisions which are important for Europe. Russia wants to be treated as an equal partner since it sees itself as part of Europe. Moreover, in the early beginnings of the EU, Russia was opposed to some EU policies. In 1995, the Schengen Agreement led to the elimination of borders within the Schengen Area. Russia, however, claimed that this would not only strengthen the border towards Russia and would thus divide European countries from Russia, but it would also violate Russia´s sovereignty and the freedom of movement for Russia´s citizens. The reasons is that Kaliningrad lies within the EU, but belongs to the Russian Federation. Hence, a free movement from one Russian territory to another Russian territory would not be possible. Even though Russia has greater contact and more agreements with the EU than with any other organization, Russia was always skeptical about EU enlargement. It is concerned with EU-NATO relations because NATO could immensely influence EU policies. Russia makes clear that the critical point in this aspect is that the US is a member of NATO, thus the US could steer EU policies through EU-NATO relations. For Russia counts, the less the Common Security and Defense Policy of the EU is influenced by the US, the better. Here, the rivalry between the US and Russia becomes obvious. Even though one could argue that the EU is not as threatening to Russia as NATO, EU enlargement remains critical for Russia since security policies often overlap. In the specific case of Ukraine, Russia has its own security policy. With EU enlargement, the EU now also developed its own security policies towards Ukraine, for example through Belarus which is Ukraine´s and Russia´s neighbor. The traditional way of thinking of Russia, which is Realpolitik, becomes clear again because to Russia, geopolitics is crucial, Ukraine is in the sphere of Commonwealth of Independent States and therefore under Russian influence. Russia´s influence on Ukraine is challenged due to EU enlargement. Furthermore, the EU created in 2004 a policy towards its new neighbors, called the European Neighborhood Policy in order to promote development and stability. To the EU, this is vital because stability within the neighboring countries would also lead to stability throughout the region. To Russia, this policy means EU interference into Russia´s sphere of influence. Ukraine developed security relations with EU members to achieve stable and secure common borders. Additionally, Ukraine tried to meet the Copenhagen Criteria in order to be able to join the EU as a member. Russia is opposed this development through which Ukraine would distance itself from Russia while having closer ties to the EU (Allison, R. et al., 2006). After the end of the Cold

War, Russia tried to convince its neighboring countries to have more integration in the region. In 2010, Russia, Belarus and Kazakhstan established the Eurasian Customs Union and in 2015, Armenia and Kyrgyzstan joined the Union. So far, the organization is not a full Customs Union yet, but the member countries are moving towards a customs union by abolishing tariffs between them and by creating a common external tariff. The Customs Union is represented by a supranational authority, the Eurasian Economic Commission. Even though Russia is the leading actor in the development of the Union, Russia and its member states claim that they have joined the Union voluntarily. Additionally, the member states argue that this organization has a pure economic character of integration. However, some scholars say that Russia wants to be an equal partner on the global stage and believes it could only be an equal partner by having control over its neighbors and by establishing a Customs Union. The Customs Union is built on foundations comparable to the ones of the EU. Russia sees the potential and success of the EU and wishes this for its own region. Russia tries to convince Ukraine to join the Union. That way, Russia would get Ukraine closer to itself and further away from the EU. In 2010, Russian president Putin promised former Ukrainian president Yanukovych that Ukraine would get cheaper Russian gas, Ukrainian´s GDP would increase and the Ukraine would have a better position when negotiating with the EU if Ukraine joins the Eurasian Customs Union (Shumylo-Tapiola, O., 2012). One might go further and argue that Russia was pressuring Ukraine to join the Union because Russia´s geopolitical interests in Ukraine are so important. Ukraine was negotiating with the EU for years about closer cooperation and former Ukrainian president Yanukovych declared to sign the EU Association Agreement. However, Putin offered Ukraine $15 billion in loans and cheaper Russian gas supply. Afterwards, Yanukovych said that he would not sign the EU Association Agreement. Mass demonstrations in Kiev followed, many Ukrainians were upset with the president´s decision (Van Herpen, M., 2014). With the EU Association Agreement, Ukraine and the EU would cooperate closely on political, economic and security aspects. Thus, it is a political and economic association with the aim to assimilate towards European Union Common Security and Defense Policy. Ukraine would need to commit to certain reforms but Ukraine would get comprehensive support (EU External Action, 2014). Many Ukrainian citizens were supporting the agreement. They hoped that with the help of the EU, they could fight corruption. They claimed that Yanukovych would not want a change, but the people do. They made the current government responsible for Ukrainians poor economic situation. Furthermore, many of the Ukrainian population saw the agreement as a basis for Ukrainian democracy which would end the authoritarian regime (Walker, S., 2014). The problem is not only that Ukraine is caught in the middle between the EU or NATO and Russia. Furthermore, Ukraine is being pushed to decide whether its policies and actions are western or Russian-oriented. The senior researcher at the Uppsala Centre of Russian Studies at the Uppsala University argues that Ukraine was being pushed into deciding of either having closer ties with the EU or Russia and its Eurasian Custom Union (Simons, G. 2015). EU Commissioner for Enlargement and Neighborhood Policy, Stefan Füle, made clear that the establishment of a free trade zone between Ukraine and the EU would be incompatible with a Ukrainian membership of the Eurasian Customs Union. He argued that this would not be based on ideological, but legal reasons. Ukraine could not decrease its customs tariffs due to the EU Association Agreement and at the same time increase its customs tariffs because it is also a member of the Eurasian Customs Union. Ukraine would have to be sovereign and decide by itself over its own trade policies when it ratifies the EU Association Agreement, this would not be the case if Ukraine would also be a member of the Eurasian Customs Union. However, there are other possibilities Ukraine could take into account for closer ties with the Union or its individual members while also having ratified the EU Association Agreement … It may certainly be possible for members of the Eastern Partnership to increase their cooperation with the Customs Union, perhaps as observers; and participation in a DCFTA is of course fully compatible with our partners' existing free trade agreements with other Commonwealth of Independent States (CIS) states. Let me be clear: the development of the Eurasian Economic Union project must respect our partners' sovereign decisions. Any threats from Russia linked to the possible signing of agreements with the European Union are unacceptable. This applies to all forms of pressure, including: the possible misuse of energy pricing … " (Füle, S., 2014). At least, on this issue, the EU and Russia have the same opinion. Russian president Putin stated that Russia would respect a country's sovereignty. However, Ukraine is integrated into the Commonwealth of Independent States which would further strive towards free trade in this area. To Ukraine, the states of the Customs Union are crucial since 30% of Ukrainian exports go to the Customs Union. In 2011, the Commonwealth of Independent States introduced an agreement for free trade. Putin argues that Ukraine would have insisted on signing this agreement. The EU Association Agreement would not be compatible with the Customs Union for legal and technical reasons. The EU would have different regulations than the Customs Union. The EU might have regulations which are not compatible with the Customs Union's regulation. Thus, a Russian good might not be allowed on the Ukrainian market. Putin states that "… We understand our European partners; they have already developed the Ukrainian market rather well, and would like to get hold of whatever is left and squeeze out everyone else". If Ukraine signs the EU Association Agreement, then Russia would treat Ukraine as a regular trading partner with no preferences which it now enjoys due to the Commonwealth of Independent States free trade zone regulations (Putin, V., 2014). Even though Ukraine is not an official member of the Commonwealth of Independent States nor is it a member of the Eurasian Customs Union, Russia certainly treats Ukraine like it would be a member by interfering into Ukrainian´s decision of either signing the EU Association Agreement or not. One could say that again, the real reasons behind Russia´s behavior are geopolitical ones. Ukraine would benefit more from being an EU member than being a member of the Customs Union. One could say that Putin is trying to re-establish Russian control over former Soviet states through economic integration, which results in spill-over effects. Hence, Russia would have political control of those states. For some, this can be the only reason why Putin offered so much money to former Ukrainian president Yanukovych if Ukraine would join the Customs Union. Especially since Russia´s own economic situation is fairly poor and economically, it would not benefit a lot from Ukraine as a trading partner. Russia also made such promises to Belarus and Armenia (Van Herpen, M., 2014). It seems that both Russia and the EU are looking for cooperation with states of the former Soviet Union through economic integration, however their motivation is rather due to political reasons. Neither side has come up with comprehensive solutions before the Ukrainian crisis. Neither side tried to openly address the other side´s concern via negotiations. Thus, it was up to Ukraine to decide which side to join. In March 2014, the new Ukrainian president Poroshenko signed the EU Association Agreement and was therewith rejecting Putin´s offer to join the Eurasian Economic Union. With this agreement, a Deep and Comprehensive Free Trade Area is planned to be established between the EU and Ukraine. This will hopefully result in comprehensive modernization of Ukraine which are based on reforms and shared values. Hence, it is not only an economic agreement but also a political association. With Russia´s annexation of Crimea, the US and the EU punished Russia for violating international law through sanctions. Russia responded with sanctions against states of the former Soviet Union which signed the EU Association Agreement, these are Ukraine, Moldova and Georgia. However, Belarus and Kazakhstan did not follow Russia. Instead, Russia acted unilaterally and this may violate the regulations of the Eurasian Economic Union and could harm the relation among the members. It could be the case that geopolitics is more important to Russia than economic integration whereas the EU values economic integration as more important than geopolitics. The result is that both conflicting sides do not understand each other, one side arguing in terms of Realpolitik and the other side arguing for liberal policies, economic integration and free trade. Russia and the EU find it difficult to find a solution because each side has their own priority and they do not want to make any sacrifices (Kansikas, S. and Palonkorpi, M. 2015). Besides the competing interests, both the EU and Russia accuse each other of interfering into Ukrainian domestic politics. It is obvious that Russia did interfere into Ukraine´s internal affairs by annexing Crimea and supporting pro-Russian separatists. However, Putin argues that Russia had to annex Crimea because Yanukovych´s removal from his position of presidency and setting up a new interim government, was a coup supported by NATO and the EU. Hence, Russia did not recognize the interim government but it also feared that the new government would violate minority rights which would have meant that the government would oppress the Russian minority in Ukraine. Putin stated that a coup occurred in Ukraine and Russia needed to protect the Russian-speaking minority, which mostly live in Eastern Ukraine and on Crimea. In March 2014, a referendum was held in Crimea. The result was that Crimean citizens wanted to be part of the Russian Federation, not of Ukraine. Putin claims that the procedure of the referendum was in compliance with international law (Putin, V., 2015). However, the General Assembly of the United Nations urges the member states not to recognize Crimea as part of the Russian Federation (United Nations, 2014). While the EU considers that economic integration would eventually lead to deeper political cooperation which would then lead to peace and security, Putin puts Realpolitik first by saying that economy would follow a security path. To Russia, the trigger of the Ukraine crisis was the statement that Ukraine would sign the EU Association Agreement because this would divide Ukraine and Russia (Putin, V., 2014). However, Ukraine was not an inactive actor in the crisis. While Ukraine is sovereign, it did not consider Russia´s interests its decision-making and this had a great impact on Russia´s behavior. Yet, Putin claiming that NATO promised not to expand beyond German borders in 1991, was not a written promise. One could suggest that the crisis would have escalated if the policy makers in 1991 would have written an agreement on this topic. But besides NATO, the EU is also perceived as a threat and thus, the crisis might have escalated anyway (Kansikas, S., 2015).

3.2.2. National Identity crisis in Ukraine

Most states in Europe have their own national identity by now which developed within the last hundred years. Many empires emerged and fell apart later on. This is also true for the Russian Empire. Ukraine was under the control of the Russian Empire for about 200 years and struggled for independence. Ukrainians identified themselves as Europeans rather than as Russians. Citizens of Ukraine were oppressed by the Russian Empire, the Russian Tsar controlled its empire and gave only little autonomy to the borderlands, which included Ukraine. The Bolsheviks in 1922 firstly supported national self-determination, but only to get public support for the fight against the authoritarian regime. Later, the Soviets oppressed any national uprising with force and introduced "Russification". National languages, symbols and rituals were banned and people were forced to learn and speak Russian. Ukraine, however, already had its own language before. It does not differ a lot from Russian, but there is a difference. It already developed its own printing press and Ukrainian traditional and culture was important to Ukrainians. During the time of the Soviet Union, Ukraine was separated from the West since it was a member of the Soviet Union. During this time, Ukraine was heavily influenced by the Russians because Moscow controlled the entire Soviet Union. With the collapse of the Soviet Union in 1991, Ukraine was able to declare its independence. Like other former states of the Soviet Union, it had to find its place in the world and needed to decide what kind of political system it would follow. The Orange Revolution in 2004 showed that a majority of Ukrainians preferred stronger ties to the EU than to Russia. They demanded democracy and wanted their government to set the path towards EU integration. However, Ukrainians in the eastern parts have family ties in Russia and were rather Pro-Russia. The eastward expansion of the EU seemed to disrupt former borders of the Soviet Union. Yet, it did set a way for Ukrainian determination, to come back to its European roots and demand its benefits it has by having European ties. Many Ukrainians see politics which is EU-oriented as cleaner and less corrupt than Russia´s politics. Others, fear that they lose their ties with Russia when Ukraine would become a rather EU-oriented state, claiming that Ukraine was and is called "Little Russia" for a reason. In the 19th century, Ukraine was heavily influenced by Poland, and Ukrainian movements arose in order to break out of the Russian Empire. The majority of Ukrainians were against the Tsar and Moscow´s control over Ukraine. They knew about the French Revolution, European liberalism was important for them as well as local history and folklore. In fact, West Ukraine was also influenced by the Austrian monarchy in which its people enjoyed a certain freedom and certain rights, more than Ukrainians or Russians enjoyed in the Russian Empire. Ukrainians were seeking reforms, demanded national rights and autonomy from the Russian Empire. It was against the authoritarian regime of the Tsar and the single control by Moscow. Thus, many Ukrainians were rather European-oriented than Russian-oriented. The Civil War in 1917 resulted in Polish occupation of West Ukraine and Russian occupation of East Ukraine. Again, the country was divided and the different influence it received had an impact on Ukraine as a nation. (Rewarkowicz, M. and Zalesko Onyshkevych, L., 2009). With the collapse of the Soviet Union, some scholars thought Ukraine would break up, mainly because of its Ukrainian-speaking people in the west and Russian-speaking people in the east. With its independence in 1991, Ukraine was not a democratic state, it did not break up but it remained one state. However, Ukraine suffered due to corruption and its negative economic situation. In 2004, the Orange Revolution followed during the presidential election. The election was marked with corruption, electoral fraud and voter intimidation. Ukrainian citizens stood up for their rights, protested and demanded freedom, human rights and democracy. Ukraine was within these events even supported by its western neighbors, such as Poland. However, the Orange Revolution did not solve the question of how the Ukrainians government should be set up and with which country it should have strong relations and cooperation. Certainly, Russia helped to dissolute the Soviet Union peacefully, this was under Gorbachev and it helped Ukraine to gain independence. However, this seems to change whenever there is a new Russian president. Putin interfered into Ukrainians internal affairs when the Orange Revolution occurred and he went even further when Russia annexed Crimea and intervened into Ukraine by supporting Ukrainian separatists. This was possible for Russia because Ukraine was not united and therefore not strong enough to stand up against unwished foreign interference. While this is true, the issue is more complex. Ukraine is divided into East and West, of course not with clear cut lines, but historically the eastern part of Ukraine was under different influence than the western part and vice versa. This also had a great impact on the political culture. Western parts of Ukraine have different values and norms than eastern regions of the country. However, the political culture affects all areas of a country and all areas of the citizens, like education, political orientation and mass media. Thus, the difference between people from east and west Ukraine is not so much about ethnicity or language, but rather about social and political aspects. This is also true about the difference between Ukrainians, especially from western regions, and Russians. Ukrainians have a different relationship towards their government than Russians towards the Russian government. Yet, this does not mean that linguistical differences are not important. They are important and this is especially true for Crimea. Crimea was part of Russia longer than other Western or Eastern Ukrainians parts. Thus, Crimean people feel close to Russia. Russian-speaking people feared that Ukrainian nationalism would arise with a changing regime and that the Russian-minority would lose its rights when the parliament started to question the status of the Russian as a minority language under the pro-European government. 17% ethnic Russians live in Ukraine, dominantly in the Eastern parts of Ukraine. Furthermore, eastern parts of Ukraine feels close to Russia for economic reasons. There is heavy industry in the east of Ukraine and they make mostly business with Russians. Hence, the Ukraine is divided by competing interests and values and has difficulty of finding its national identity which would unite them (Kutsch, T., 2014).

4. Who is to blame for the Ukraine crisis and does finger-pointing make sense to solve the crisis?

Scholar J.J. Mearsheimer argues that the set-up of sanctions by the US against Russia had the effect of escalating the crisis because with this movement, the US shows that it is involved in the crisis, even though it should not be. Moreover, the US does not recognize its own responsibility in the crisis and claims that all responsibility lays with Russian president Putin. However, Putin is only one actor in the crisis. His actions of annexing Crimea were violating international law but one needs to understand why Russia did what it did in order to undertake actions to ease the situation and to find solutions. To Russia, geopolitics and Realpolitik is important, but the US thinks differently and thus, ignores Russia´s interests. Furthermore, it was wrong by the US to support the Euromaidan protests because this was provocative for Russia and made the crisis worse. It was also a mistake by the US and EU to set up a not only a pro-Western government but an anti-Russian government which was by Putin perceived as an attack against Russia and against its geopolitical interests. Mearsheimer states that the ignorance of geopolitical interests by the US is paradox since the US perceives its Monroe Doctrine as very important. The Monroe Doctrine contains that inference into internal US affairs will be perceived as a threat of aggression and intervention. Hence, the US should that Russia perceives US, EU or NATO interference into Ukrainian affairs as a threat of intervention which Russia wants to prevent (Mearsheimer, J.J., 2015). However, other scholars countered Mearsheimer´s arguments saying that NATO expansion cannot explain Russia´s aggression in Ukraine because NATO mostly expanded eastwards in 1999 and 2004 but Russia did not act in response until 2014 with its annexation of Crimea and interference into Ukraine. Moreover, Putin never clearly mentioned that NATO expansion would be a threat. Before 2014, there was a rather good relationship between US and Russia. The focus was on cooperation in, for example, Afghanistan and Syria and the signing of the New START Treaty. Furthermore, neither NATO nor the Ukrainian government had NATO membership for Ukraine on their agenda. It was rather Russia´s politics that changed when Putin tended to lose his legitimacy as a president. Thus, he influenced Russian media with propaganda and made the US responsible for issues within Russia. With this, the US was perceived by the Russian public as an enemy. Putin claimed to protect Russia´s national interests against Western countries and the result was that he gained popularity among Russians. Moreover, Putin claimed that a coup occurred when former Ukrainian president Yanukovych was removed and replaced. Scholars argue that this was not true because Yanukovych lost his legitimacy quickly when he declared he would not sign the EU Association Treaty. Demonstrations followed and he was removed by the parliament, not by the

EU or the US. Hence, it was not a coup, but Putin needed to label the event as one because he saw Ukraine turning towards the EU and the US. The crisis is therefore not about NATO, the EU or the US, but about Putin himself. He tried to hide Russia's military involvement in the crisis, he acted irrationally and out of impulses. He did not demonstrate Russia's national interest but his own political desires. However, even though Putin violated international law, the US and the EU also share responsibilities of the crisis. Currently, it should not be about NATO membership for Ukraine and it should also not be about geopolitics, but the most important aspect now is to hold Ukraine together which should be in the interest of all actors. For this, all countries have to work together (McFaul, M. and Sestanovich, S., 2015). Analyzing the different views scholars have on who is mostly responsible and to blame for the Ukraine crisis and seeing that the views differ clarify that finger-pointing is not a solution to the crisis. It rather makes the crisis worse. Hence, it is important to deal with the current situation the way it is.

5. What needs to be done to solve the Ukraine crisis

When analyzing the crisis, one can see that different scholars see different origins of the crisis which makes solving the crisis difficult. So far, Russia annexed Crimea and fights are continuing in eastern regions of Ukraine, especially in Donetsk and Luhansk. Pro-Russian separatists are fighting for independence from Ukraine and a further step would be to join the Russian Federation. Kiev´s army tries to defend Ukraine and its citizens. As the fight goes on, many people die. In September 2014, a ceasefire was introduced through the Minsk Agreement which was negotiated by Ukrainians Government representatives, and separatist leaders. Russian representatives as well representatives of the OSCE monitored the procedure. The main points of the agreement were that there should be a ceasefire and that Ukrainians territorial integrity and sovereignty has to be respected (Walker, S., 2014). However, the agreement was violated. Russia claims that the Ukrainian government, which already came into power under unconstitutional circumstances due to coup, would send its army and use military force, including heavy weapons, against eastern parts of Ukraine. This led to causalities and many refugees are migrating to Russia (Kelin, A., 2014). In contrast, the Ukrainian government argues that Russia and Pro-Russian separatists in Ukraine violated the Minsk agreement by continuing their attacks against Ukrainian cities. Russia would support the separatists with heavy weaponry. Moreover, separatists in Donetsk and Luhansk held a referendum claiming the result was that people in those regions demand independence and further steps for integration into the Russian Federation. The EU and the Ukrainian government claims that the elections were illegal and therefore would violate the Minsk agreement which states that peace for eastern Ukraine should occur by respecting Ukraine´s sovereignty and territorial integrity (Prokopchuk, I., 2014). Russia denies to deliver weapons to separatists in Donetsk and Luhansk. The US and EU were debating about sending military assistance to Ukraine to strengthen its currently weak army and to defend Ukraine against the aggression by separatists and Russia. Whether Western countries should send military aid to Ukraine or not is a highly controversial topic. The EU tries to solve the conflict with diplomatic means, saying that military force would not solve the conflict in the long-term and could make the conflict even worse (Schmemann, S., 2015). Many scholars are in favor of the EU and US sending military aid to Ukraine, because only then Ukraine would be able to defend itself against Russian aggression. So far, the EU and the US hoped that sanctions against Russia would stop Russia´s attack against Ukraine and its support to separatists and that sanctions would push Russia to accept the negotiated agreements. Instead, Putin still supports separatists, violates the Minsk agreement and separatists try to get more

Ukrainian territory under their control. The US and the EU fear that lethal aid would result in an escalation of Russia´s aggression. However, even though the EU and the US did not send military aid to Ukraine yet, Russia still supports separatists, attacks cities and Russia´s aggression escalates. Thus, many people say it is time to send military aid to Ukraine because not sending it made the situation escalate and separatists seized more territory. Currently, the US and NATO debate about what kind of defensive military aid should be sent to Ukraine. US President Obama, however, is still not willing to send weapons. Scholars argue that Putin would only try to solve the conflict with diplomatic means when war and aggression get too costly for Russia, and this would be the case if Ukraine´s military is backed up with Western military aid. If Putin was interested of solving the conflict with diplomatic means, then he have tried to convince separatists to stop attacking cities and he would have stopped to provide weapons to them. Instead he violated the Minsk Agreement, which was a diplomatic solution. Furthermore, the Minsk Agreement from September 2014 contained many aspects Putin demanded, but he still violated the agreement. This could be a sign that he is not interested in diplomatic solutions. If he would not have violated the agreement, Ukraine would not have wanted to join NATO but since it constantly fears to be faced with Russian aggression, it has to seek NATO membership. Sanctions and agreements did not help to prevent further escalations of the conflict, military aid for Ukraine would made the Ukrainian army stronger and it would be able to protect Ukraine from Russia and its separatists. War would be then too costly for Putin, so Russia would have to be committed to agreement (Rubin, T., 2015). However, opinions tend to differ on the topic. Many scholar claim that Western military support of Ukraine would be perceived as a war declaration by Russia. Thus, the conflict would escalate, maybe even on a global scale. Especially if the US would support Ukraine militarily, then the US would be directly involved in the conflict and Russia would respond to this. Russia could even respond with a proxy war, like in times of the Cold War, to present its power. It could be that Russia would then not only further support separatists but it would also attack other fronts. Furthermore, sending weapons to Ukraine can have unintended consequences. Since the Ukrainian military suffers from corruption, weapons sent by the EU and the US might get stolen and sold, they might end up in the hands of separatists (Bodner, M. 2015). Even though, the US did not send weapons to Ukraine yet, it passed a bill in September 2014 called the Ukraine Freedom Support Act. The Support Act states that tougher sanctions on Russia will be imposed by the US and the US would provide military assistance like weapons and training. Furthermore, the US provides financial aid to Ukraine in order to counter propaganda by Russia. Moreover, Ukraine received the status as a major non-NATO ally. The goal of the bill is to re-establish Ukrainian sovereignty and territorial integrity (US Senate Committee on Foreign Relations, 2014). The EU, on the other hand, still tries to solve the conflict with diplomacy only. German chancellor Merkel and French president Hollande met first with Ukrainian president Poroshenko and then with Russian president Putin to negotiate a further ceasefire and the implementation of the Minsk agreement. On 12th of February 2015, the leaders of Germany, France, Ukraine and Russia came to an agreement. The ceasefire will start on 15th of February 2015, this is the date Russian president Putin demanded even though Ukrainian president Poroshenko argued for an immediate ceasefire. People argue that the additional days would give Russia and the separatists more time to seize Ukrainian territory. Ukraine and Russia agreed on taking out their heavy weapons from Eastern Ukraine and withdrawing their fighters. Russia´s agreement to this was surprising since president Putin always claimed that there would be no Russian forces in Ukraine and that Russia would not support separatists. The agreement furthermore states that Ukraine will have full control over eastern Ukraine, local elections will be held and constitutional changes will allow those regions more autonomy (The Editorial Board, 2015). For future actions, it is important that neither the US, the EU nor Russia tries to influence Ukraine, they should rather find a "common language" in order to solve the crisis and hold Ukraine together (Vasecka, M., 2015). Important is to re-introduce international law and territorial integrity. The crisis should only be solved through diplomatic means and NATO has to consider its participation in Ukraine carefully since it is perceived as a threat by Russia and it is Russia´s former enemy. Thus, NATO has to act sensibly. It is crucial to try everything to avoid provocations towards Russia but it is necessary to punish Russia for its violation of international law. Best punishments are sanctions which will result in consequences desired by the EU and the US. The conflict will be soon too costly for Russia and it has to change its behavior. Hence, the Ukraine crisis would not result in a new Cold War, in a sense of competing interests of nuclear powers with a real global threat to all countries. Furthermore, there should be no military intervention or military support by foreign countries since they have unintended consequences, the crisis would escalate and more innocent people would be killed (Bergmann, G., 2015). Yet, other experts seem to be rather pessimistic about the crisis and its outcome, seeing the Ukraine crisis as a crisis worse than the Cold War and Russia as an absolute aggressor which is difficult to stop "… combination of the worse traditions of the Soviet Union, Czarist Russia, Russian orthodox church, Ivan ´The Terrible´ times with ´oprichniky´ and altogether framed in a quasi-modern state that is shisoprhenically balancing between feelings of superiority and humiliating feelings of being average…" (Vasecka,M., 2015).

6. Conclusion

After analyzing various arguments of what the trigger was for the Ukraine crisis to escalate, who is to blame for it and what has to be done in order to solve the crisis, different opinions and solutions exists which tend to differ extremely. This was not only obvious when I was researching and analyzing literature review but also when I was doing interviews with four different interview partners. Finding out to what extend the views of scholars on this topic differ, let us only assume that the involved parties might have even more extreme different views. This makes it very difficult to find a common language and a solution for the crisis. Finger-pointing and blaming states and its actors is thus not helpful to find a solution to the crisis. This would only result in more arguments and more fights. Russia will only change its behavior if western countries change their behavior and vice versa. Yet, Russia will continue to feel threatened by NATO and EU expansion and will therefore continue to prevent its national interests through military means. There is nothing that western countries could do right now to convince Russia that it does not have to feel threatened. It is now up to the west to find a solution. This is not because Russia is right with its arguments or because its actions are justified. Russia is behaving aggressively, inappropriately and it is violating international law. However, the hypothesis that Realpolitik still matters was verified. To which degree Realpolitik has to be considered varies with the different leaders, especially those of Ukraine and Russia. In the end of the Cold War, Russia had a rather liberal and western-oriented leader, Gorbachev, who found a common language with its European and US collegues. To Gorbachev, democracy and freedom was more important than Realpolitik and geopolitics. Yet, with the end of the Cold War, Russia lost the control of its neighbors. The result was that geopolitics mattered again and Russia became concerned about its neighbors and its weak influence on them. As mentioned above, Russian president Putin argued that the collapse of the Soviet Union was a geopolitical catastrophe and Russia´s national interests are high on the agenda of Russian foreign policy. When reading Putin´s statements, it is obvious that Russia still has not found its place on the international stage. It was a powerful regime for many years and today Russia feels that it is not treated as an equally powerful partner anymore. Within this lays the trigger of the current Ukraine crisis. With the demise of Russia´s influence, Realpolitik became important again. Putin did not feel to be able to participate properly in influential organizations like NATO or the EU. The result was that Russia was not satisfied with the post- Cold War situation. Even though NATO and the EU set up several agreements with Russia to ensure that neither of them had the will to gain more influence in former Soviet Union states and that neither of them had the intention to threaten Russia, this did not guarantee that Russia's national interests will be protected. When the EU and NATO expanded, Putin stated that Russia was oppose such expansions. It is clear that Russia follows Realpolitik because it does not trust other states and prefers to act unilaterally and even violates international law in order to protect its survival and geopolitical interests. NATO and EU implemented their last expansions some years ago, but Russia acted in 2014 because it saw its influence on former soviet states, namely Ukraine, as taken away when Ukrainian president Yanukovych declared to sign the EU Association Agreement. Russia was not able to push Ukraine into being a member of the Commonwealth of Independent States or into being a member of the newly created Eurasian Economic Union. All these organizations are labeled as economic and political integration, but in fact, Russia tries to gain back its control over former Soviet Union states. At this point, I need to make clear that Russia's action, such as the annexation of Crimea, supporting separatists with weapons and intervening in Ukraine, are violations against international law and cannot be justified for any reason. However, it is important to try understand Russia's action in order to prevent further aggression. States and non-state actors do not have to understand Putin's actions on moral or legal grounds, but they have to analyze them in order to be able to act appropriately. The EU, the US and NATO have to understand that Realpolitik still matters. With this, it is not important to argue if Realpolitik is wrong or not, but it is important to accept that it still matters for some states. If western countries do not accept it, then they ignore important messages, which Putin stated in several speeches, and will then be surprised if Putin responds aggressively. Putin's behavior is aggressive but western states need to do everything to avoid provocations. Since there is no higher authority above states, aggressive behavior and provocation have to be avoided. In the end, Russia belongs to the international system and western countries will have to deal with Russia, especially in times of globalization, whether it wants to or not. Hence, it is important to deal with the crisis with diplomatic means. It is understandable that Ukraine wishes to defend itself. However, military aid in terms of lethal aid can have unintended consequence which could worsen the situation in Ukraine. More innocent people could get killed, the weapons could end up in the hands of separatists and since the Ukrainian army is corruptive, soldiers might sale the weapons. Furthermore, it could also lead to an arms race which the world already experienced during the Cold War. Even though, this arms race would probably not be one of nuclear arms, the possibility is there. If the arms race would not be about nuclear arms, then it would be about heavy weaponry which is also counterproductive to finding a solution to the crisis. Moreover, lethal aid by foreign countries could result in a proxy-war which the world also experienced during the Cold War. Then, the conflict would not be about Ukraine itself but about competing views. Hence, the crisis can only be solved through diplomatic means like sanctions. Sanctions have already affected Russia´s economy and even though Putin will try to spend as much money on Russia´s military as possible, this will no longer be possible when Russia faces serious financial issues. Continuous agreements, talks and sanctions will push Putin to commit to international law, to convince separatists to stop the attacks and it will lead Russia to withdraw its soldiers from Ukraine. Yet, Russia is not the only actor responsible in this crisis. The Ukrainian government is an active actor which has to ensure to commit to minority rights. This would ease the relation between Ukraine and its population in eastern Ukraine. Organizations like the OSCE, Amnesty International are responsible to monitor this. For future peace in Ukraine, international organizations play an important role. If the Ukrainian government would violate minority rights, then it is up to those organizations to stop violations and oppression. However, here it is important that Russia will trust international organizations again. So far, Russia felt that it could not participate in the decision-making of NATO and EU properly. Russia will only trust that other states would decide correctly when Russian minority rights are violated in Ukraine if the EU, the US and NATO will not interfere into the internal affairs of Ukraine. This does not mean that if Russia violates international law, like it did when it annexed Crimea or intervened into Ukraine, Russia will be unpunished. Here again, imposing sanctions is important. Key to the solution of the crisis in Ukraine is that western countries do not have to completely understand why Realpolitik is important to some countries, they rather just have to accept that Realpolitik still matters to some countries, like Russia. Hence, they have to act accordingly. Diplomatic means are the only solution because multilateral agreements, or bilateral which are monitored by third parties, ensure that international law is not violated. Unilateral behavior always contains the risk that other countries perceive this unilateral action as imperialistic action or aggressive behavior. Even though NATO and EU are international organizations, western countries have to accept that Russia perceives those organizations as a threat, they do not have to understand Russia´s fears but they have to consider them. This does not mean that a sovereign state which belonged to the Soviet Union before and thus was under Russian control, cannot be a member of NATO or the EU in the future. However, one must deal with these topics very sensibly. Not because Russia´s fears are understandable but because they exist and western countries cannot change it soon. This means that even though Ukraine is sovereign, the Ukrainian government has to do a cost-benefit analysis and has to try to avoid risks. This could mean that Ukraine cannot be a member of the EU or NATO as long as Russia feels threatened by these actions. Otherwise Ukraine would need to expect further aggressions by Russia. Ukraine might feel that it cannot exercise its sovereign rights, but in the end, the protection of the Ukrainian population should be the most important aspect and this can mean that Ukraine has to compromise or sacrifice. Furthermore, the US and the EU should not support a government which is extremely anti-Russian, they should rather support a moderate Ukrainian government which does commits to minority rights and honors diversity. Hence, the Russian minority in Ukraine would feel more secure and would not support separatists. It is important to strengthen Ukraine as a nation and to hold it together. If the population feels safe, then it is also immunized against Russian propaganda and it will be able to protect itself against external influences. Solving the crisis with diplomatic means instead of military means does not mean that western countries give in and Russia can do what it wishes to do, it rather means that western states try to avoid a worst-case scenario which would be a new Cold War. This way of ending the crisis may not result in finding the perfect solution but since the crisis is very complex, it is about finding the best solution western states have given certain options. This solution has the main consequence of avoiding further escalation while putting Russia back on the track of international law.

References

Allison, R., et al. (2006) Russian security engagement with NATO, Putin´s Russia and the Enlarged Europe, Chatham House, pp. 94 - 116

Allison, R., et al. (2006) Russian security engagement with the European Union, Putin´s Russia and the Enlarged Europe, Chatham House, pp. 72 - 91

Arun, S. (2015) The Return of Realpolitik, The Diplomatc, Available from http://thediplomat.com/2015/01/thereturnofrealpolitik/ [Accessed on 06.02.2015]

Ashton, C. (2013), State by EU High Representative Catherine Ashton on Ukraine, European External Action Service, Available from http://www.eeas.europa.eu/statements/docs/2013/131121_04_en.pdf [Accessed 02.01.15]

Baczynska, G. et al (2014), Pushing locals aside, Russians take top rebel posts in east Ukraine, Reuters, Available from http://www.reuters.com/article/2014/07/27/us-ukraine-crisis-rebels-insight-idUSKBN0FW07020140727 [Accessed 02.01.15]

Balmforth, R. (2013), Kiev protestors gather, EU dangles aid promise, Reuters, Available from http://www.reuters.com/article/2013/12/12/us-ukraine-idUSBRE9BA04420131212 [Accessed 02.01.15]

BBC (2014), Ukraine profile, Available from http://www.bbc.com/news/world-europe-18010123 [Accessed 02.01.15]

BBC (2013), Ukraine suspends preparations for EU trade agreement, Available from http://www.bbc.com/news/world-europe-25032275 [Accessed 02.01.15]

BBC (2013), Ukraine unrest: Protestors blockade government sites, Available from http://www.bbc.com/news/world-europe-25180502 [Accessed 02.01.15]

BBC (2014), EU signs pact with Ukraine, Georgia and Moldova, Available from http://www.bbc.com/news/world-europe-28052645 [Accessed 02.01.15]

BBC (2014), Ukrainian Crisis: Timeline, Available from http://www.bbc.com/news/world-middle-east-26248275 [Accessed 02.01.15]

Bergmann, Günther (2015) Interviewed by Nadine O'Shea.

Berkley Center (2014), Leonid Kravchuk, Available from http://berkleycenter.georgetown.edu/people/leonid-kravchuk [Accessed 02.01.15]

Birnbaum, M. et al (2014), In Ukrainian presidential election, chocolate tycoon Poroshenko claims victory, The Washington Pot, Available from http://www.washingtonpost.com/world/ukrainians-head-to-the-polls-to-elect-a-new-president-except-in-the-restive-east/2014/05/25/2680fad4-e9f7-4118-923e-852b01351b39_story.html [Accessed 02.01.15]

Black, J.L. (2004), Ukraine and Belarus, Vladimir Putin and the New World Order, Rowman & Littlefield Publisher, pp. 247 – 251

Bodner, M. (2015) Russia Would See US Moves to Arm Ukraine as Declaration of War, the Moscow Times, Available from http://www.themoscowtimes.com/business/article/u-s-military-aid-to-ukraine-would-be-declaration-of-proxy-war-russian-defense-analysts/515654.html [Accessed on 14.02.2015]

Bowen, A.S. and Galeotti, M. (2014) Putin´s Empire of the Mind, Foreign Policy (May/June 2014), pp. 16 - 19

Campbell, C. (2013), U.S. Intelligence: It's Looking More Likely That Russia Will Invade Ukraine, Time, Available from http://time.com/39705/russia-invasion-ukraine-likely/ [Accessed 02.01.15]

Consulate General of Ukraine in New York (2007), Basic Facts about Ukraine, Available from http://www.ukrconsul.org/BASIC_FACTS.htm [Accessed 01.01.15)

European Court of Human Rights (2013), Case of Tymoshenko vs. Ukraine, Available from http://hudoc.echr.coe.int/sites/eng/Pages/search.aspx#{"fulltext":["tymoshenko"],"documentcollectionid2":["GRANDCHAMBER","CHAMBER"],"itemid":["001-119382"]} [Accessed 02.01.15]

EU External Action (2014) EU-Ukrainian Association Agreement, European Commission, Available from http://eeas.europa.eu/images/top_stories/140912_eu-ua_aa_what_does_the_agreement_offer_v.pdf [Accessed on 08.02.2015]

Füle, S. (2014) Statement on the pressure exercised by Russia on countries of the Eastern Partnership, European Commission, Available from http://europa.eu/rapid/press-release_SPEECH-13-687_en.htm [Accessed on 08.02.2015]

German Ministry of Foreign Affairs (2014), Ukraine, Available from http://www.auswaertiges-amt.de/DE/Aussenpolitik/Laender/Laenderinfos/01-Nodes_Uebersichtsseiten/Ukraine_node.html [Accessed 01.01.15]

German Parliament (2014), Bundeskanzlerin Merkel telefoniert mit dem russischen Präsidenten Wladimit Putin, Available from http://www.bundesregierung.de/Content/DE/Pressemitteilungen/BPA/2014/03/20140331merkelputintelefonat.html [Accessed 02.01.15]

Golinkin, L. (2014), Kiev's brutal strategy in eastern Ukraine, Los Angeles Times, Available from http://www.latimes.com/opinion/op-ed/la-oe-golinkin-ukraine-humanitarian-crisis-20150102-story.html [Accessed 02.01.15]

Herszenhorn, D.M. (2014), Ukraine rushes to shift power and mend rifts, New York Times, Available from http://www.nytimes.com/2014/02/24/world/europe/ukraine.html [Accessed 02.01.15]

JENKINS, B. 2014. Crisis In Crimea: A Historical Lead Up To The Conflict Between Russia and Ukraine. *CreateSpace Independent Publishing Platform.*

Kansikas, Suvi. (2015) Interviewed by Nadine O'Shea.

Kansikas, S. and Palonkorpi, M. (2015) The EEU, the EU and the New Spheres of Influence Game in the South Caucasus, the Ministry for Foreign Affairs of Finland, pp. 197- 228

Kelin, A. (2014) Russian Permanent Representative to the OSCE, Ministry of Foreign Affairs to the Russian Federation, Available from http://www.mid.ru/brp_4.nsf/0/30F581EF951C56ADC3257DAC00683FA3 [Accessed on 13.02.2015]

Kissinger, H. (1994) *Russian and American Interests after the Cold* War Rethinking Russia's National Interests, Center for Strategic and International Studies Washington, p. 1 – 9

Kutsch, T. (2014) Ukrainians in the south and east oppose pro-Western leadership, Aljazeera America, Available from http://america.aljazeera.com/articles/2014/2/27/in-ukraine-s-eastdivisionnotdissolution.html [Accessed on 13.02.2015]

McFaul, M. and Sestanovich, S. (2015) Faulty Powers, Foreign Affairs, Available from http://www.foreignaffairs.com/articles/142260/michaelmcfaulstephensestanovichjohnjmearsheimer/Faultypowers [Accessed on 15.02.2015]

Mearsheimer, J.J. (2014) Why the Ukraine Crisis is the West's Fault, Foreign Affairs, Available from http://www.foreignaffairs.com/articles/141769/john-j-mearsheimer/why-the-ukraine-crisis-is-the-wests-fault [Accessed on 06.02.2015]

Mearsheimer, J.J. (2015) Getting Ukraine Wrong, The New York Times, Available from http://www.nytimes.com/2014/03/14/opinion/gettingukrainewrong.Html [Accessed on 15.02.2015]

Ministry of Foreign Affairs of Ukraine (2014), Protocol on the results of consultations of the Trilateral Contact Group, Available from http://mfa.gov.ua/en/news-feeds/foreign-offices-news/27596-protocolon-the-results-of-consultations-of-the-trilateral-contact-group-minsk-05092014 [Accessed 02.01.15]

Miriam Elder (2012), Ukrainians protest against Russian language law, The Guardian, Available from http://www.theguardian.com/world/2012/jul/04/ukrainians-protest-russian-language-law [Accessed 02.01.15]

Morello, C. et al. (2014), Crimea's parliament votes to join Russia, The Washington Post, Available from http://www.washingtonpost.com/world/crimeas-parliament-votes-to-join-russia/2014/03/17/5c3b96ca-adba-11e3-9627-c65021d6d572_story.html [Accessed 02.01.15]

NATO (2014) NATO's relations with Ukraine, NATO-Ukraine relations, Available from http://www.nato.int/cps/en/natohq/topics_37750.htm? [Accessed on 06.02.2015]

OECD (2013), Glossary of statistical terms, Available from http://stats.oecd.org/glossary/detail.asp?ID=392 [Accessed 01.01.15]

Patrushev, N. (2014) Cold War II: Interview with Nikolay Patrushev, Secretary of the Russian Security Council, Veterans News Now, Available from http://www.veteransnewsnow.com/2014/10/24/cold-war-ii-interview-with-nikolay-patrushev-secretary-of-the-russian-security-council/ [Accessed on 02.02.2015]

Pradetto, A. (2014) Die Krim, die bösen Russen und der empörte Westen, Blätter für Deutsche und Internationale Politik, pp. 73 – 78

Prokopchuk, I. (2014) Statement by the Delegation of Ukraine, Ministry of Foreign Affairs of Ukraine, Available from http://mfa.gov.ua/en/news-feeds/foreign-offices-news/32843-zajava-delegaciji-ukrajini-shhodo-trivajuchoji-agresiji-proti-ukrajini-z-boku-rosiji-ta-porushennya-principiv-ta-zobovjazany-v-ramkah-obse [Accessed on 13.02.2015]

Putin, W. (2001) Wortprotokoll der Rede Wladimir Putins im Deutschen Bundestag am 25.09.2001 Deutscher Bundestag, Available from http://www.bundestag.de/kulturundgeschichte/geschichte/gastredner/putin/putin_wort/244966,

Putin, W. (2007) Speech and the Following Discussion at the Munich Conference on Security Policy, Kremlin Archiv, Available from http://archive.kremlin.ru/eng/speeches/2007/02/10/0138_type82912type82914type82917type84779_118123.shtml [Accessed on 06.02.2015]

Putin, V. (2013) Presidential Adress to the Federal Assembly of the Russian Federation, The Kremlin Moscow, Available from http://eng.kremlin.ru/news/6402 [Accessed on 08.02.2015]

Putin, V. (2014) Speech at the meeting of the Customs Union, Heads of State with president of Ukraine and EU representatives, Kremlin/Moscow, Available from http://eng.kremlin.ru/transcripts/22851 [Accessed on 08.02.2015]

Putin, V. (2014) Adress by the President of the Russian Federation, The Kremlin Moscow, Available from http://eng.kremlin.ru/news/6889 [Accessed on 13.02.2015]

Putin, V. (2014) Interview to German TV channel ARD, Kremlin Moscow, Available from http://eng.kremlin.ru/news/23253 [Accessed on 13.02.2015]

Rewarkowicz, M. and Zalesko Onyshkevych, L. (2009) Contemporary Ukraine on the Cultural Map of Europe, M.E. Sharpe Inc., pp. 1 – 30

Rubin, T. (2015) Ukraine needs military aid, The Seattle Times, Available from http://seattletimes.com/html/opinion/2025586731_trudyrubincolumnukraine02xml.html [Accessed on 14.02.2015]

Rutland. P (2013), Ukraine´s Identity Crisis, [Kindle Version] Transitions Online, Chapter: Timeline, Available from http://www.amazon.com/Ukraines-Identity-Crisis-Understanding-Transitions-ebook/dp/B00HG917EG [Accessed 02.01.15]

Schmemann, S. (2015) European Leaders Debate Aid to Ukraine, but Not Russia´s Transgressions, The New York Times, Available from http://www.nytimes.com/2015/02/10/opinion/europe-leaders-debate-aid-to-ukraine-but-not-russias-transgressions.html [Accessed on 14.02.2015]

Shear, M. et al (2014), Obama Says Plane Was Shot Down From Rebel Held Ukraine Area, The New York Times, Available from http://www.nytimes.com/2014/07/19/us/obama-to-speak-about-downing-of-malaysian-plane.html [Accessed 02.01.15]

Shumylo-Tapiola, O. (2012) The Eurasian Customs Union, Carnegie Endowment for International Peace, Available from http://carnegieendowment.org/files/customs_union.pdf [Accessed on 08.02.2015]

Siddique, H. et al. (2014), Crimean parliament seizure inflames Russian-Ukrainian tensions, The Guardian, Available from http://www.theguardian.com/world/2014/feb/27/ukraine-pro-russian-gunmen-seize-crimea-parliament-live-updates [Accessed 02.01.15]

Simons, Greg. (2015) Interviewed by Nadine O'Shea.

The Editorial Board (2015) Making the Ukraine Cease-Fire Stick, The New York Times, Available from http://www.nytimes.com/2015/02/13/opinion/making-the-ukraine-cease-fire-stick.html [Accessed on 14.02.2015]

The White House (2014), *Readout of the President's Calls with President Berzins of Latvia, Prime Minister Cameron of the United Kingdom, President Grybauskaite of Lithuania, President Hollande of France, President Ilves of Estonia, and Prime Minister Renzi of Italy*, Available from http://www.whitehouse.gov/the-press-office/2014/03/08/readout-president-s-calls-president-berzins-latvia-prime-minister-camero [Accessed 02.01.15]

United Nations (2014) General Assembly Adopts Resolution Calling upon States Not to Recognize Changes in Status of Crimea Region, UN Meetings coverage and press releases, Available from http://www.un.org/press/en/2014/ga11493.doc.htm [Accessed on 13.02.2015]

US Department of State (2009) *United States Relations with Russia* Archive - Office of the Historian, Available from http://2001-2009.state.gov/r/pa/ho/pubs/fs/85965.htm [Accessed on 31.01.2015]

US Senate Committee on Foreign Relations (2014) Senate Foreign Relations Committee Unanimously Passes Ukraine Freedom Support Act of 2014, US Senate, Available from http://www.foreign.senate.gov/press/chair/release/senate-foreign-relations-committee-unanimously-passes-ukraine-freedom-support-act-of-2014 [Accessed on 14.02.2015]

Van Herpen, M. (2014) Putin´s Wars, Rowman&Littlefield, pp. 66 – 67, 62 – 85

Vasecka, Michal (2015) Interviewed by Nadine O'Shea.

Walker, S. (2014) Ukraine´s Vitali Klitschko, The Guardian, Available from http://www.theguardian.com/world/2014/jan/21/ukraine-vitali-klitschko-street-protests-corruption-interview [Accessed on 02.08.2015]

Walker, S. (2014) Ukraine ceasefire agreed for east of country at Minsk peace talks, The Gurdian, Available from http://www.theguardian.com/world/2014/sep/05/ukraine-ceasefire-east-minsk-peace-talks [Accessed on 13.02.2015]

Zadorozhny, et al (2014), Appreal from the Ukrainian Association of International Law, Cambridge Journal of International and Comparative Law, Available from http://cjicl.org.uk/2014/03/05/appeal-ukrainian-association-international-law/ [Accessed 02.01.15]

Zubok, V.M. (2007) Failed Empire: The Soviet Union in the Cold War from Stalin to Gorbachev, University of North Carolina Press, pp. 303 – 317